"I SAW THE LORD"

"I SAW THE LORD"

Joseph's First Vision Combined from Nine Accounts

KERRY MUHLESTEIN

DESERET
BOOK

Salt Lake City, Utah

To all my teachers,
from home to church to seminary to BYU to colleagues,
who have taught me about Joseph Smith.

And to my students,
who have helped me explore the story more richly.

Library of Congress Cataloging-in-Publication Data

(CIP data on file)
ISBN 978-1-62972-755-4

Printed in the United States of America
PubLitho, Draper, UT

10   9   8   7   6   5   4   3   2   1

CONTENTS

ACKNOWLEDGMENTS

I have been blessed to have extraordinary opportunities to learn about the First Vision. I cannot thank everyone who has taught me, but I would like to mention a few in particular. I will never forget my parents loading my family up in a borrowed, beat-up old motorhome and taking us to the Sacred Grove and teaching us about the First Vision there. Nor will I forget my wife, parents-in-law, and children allowing me to take them there in a beat-up old motorhome and unfold to them there the story I try to unfold here. Milton Backman and Keith Perkins were amazing in what they taught me, in book and class respectively, about this event. Steven Harper was pivotal in helping me years ago better understand and appreciate the various accounts, and in helping me put together the way I would teach the event to my classes. He also was very helpful in giving me ideas for this manuscript. Lisa

Roper was wonderful in helping me revise the story I tell here. Additionally, exploring the First Vision with my students in class after class has helped me find the richness of the accounts.

As always, my family, especially my wife, has been an inspiration to me as I have written.

INTRODUCTION

‹❧ Two hundred years ago, in the spring of 1820, Joseph Smith stepped into a grove of trees on his family farm and was blessed with a vision that changed the course of human history and mankind's interaction with God. This is as seminal an event as any that has ever happened, except for the birth, ministry, death, and Resurrection of Jesus Christ.

Joseph retold the story of that event many times, and some of his retellings were recorded. Three times he wrote down the account himself or recorded it via scribe. Several times others wrote down what he was saying, often in their journals or in the prophet's journal. Some of those who heard him tell the story in turn wrote it down in their own words to use in their missionary activities. As a result of all these efforts, we are blessed to have a tremendous amount of documentation concerning the

First Vision. No other encounter with God is as well documented as this one. What a blessing!

Each account is somewhat different. As with the retelling of any story, the details Joseph shared varied according to a host of factors, including his audience, the time he had to tell the story, what he had learned since the last time he had told it, and what seemed important to him at that stage of his life. In many cases he told the same details with very similar language, but sometimes he used slightly different language, which provides more nuance to our understanding of what happened. Additionally, each account has some details that are not in any of the other accounts. As we put all of the accounts together, we get a much fuller picture of what led up to that glorious event and what happened in that wooded area. Yet the entire story, with everything we know Joseph Smith said about it, has not been put together in one place that's easy for most members of The Church of Jesus Christ of Latter-day Saints to access.

The purpose of this little book is to make it possible for everyone to read the whole story. I have tried to write it so that the young and the mature, the well-versed member and the new convert, the passionate and the passingly curious, can all read and get something out of it. I may not have succeeded in this goal, but it has been my desire. I have tried to harmonize all the first- and secondhand accounts. It is difficult to know what details to trust when

2

reading a secondhand account. Did the person who heard Joseph tell the story remember *and* record it correctly, years later, with none of the embellishments or gap-fillers that we often use when we attempt to tell someone else's story? I have used only the details from these accounts that, to me, seem reliable.[1] This endeavor involves a certain amount of guesswork, but I have applied good historical methods, using clues that are available to us. For example, Joseph Smith himself quotes from Orson Pratt's retelling of the First Vision, making Pratt's details seem fairly reliable. Orson Hyde's account uses many of these same phrases and ideas. In other cases, certain details are emphasized strongly enough that they are also likely to be accurate.

For the most part I try to let the historical accounts tell the story. At the same time, it is helpful to think through the practicalities of the situation and take into account the historical and cultural setting. Thus I sometimes fill in gaps in the story with my own conclusions. When doing so, I alert the reader to my own editorializing by using phrases such as "must have," "likely," "certainly," or "undoubtedly." I also compare some of Joseph's experiences to those of other prophets so that we may better understand what he saw, or the experience of being transfigured. While I provide citations to let readers know

---

1. See the description of each account in Appendix A for an explanation of my method.

where the information they are reading comes from, it is safe to assume that anything included comes from the primary sources unless I use language that indicates otherwise.

I am including an appendix that outlines the various accounts and shows which details come from each account (Appendix A). Additionally, anyone who wants to can enjoy reading those accounts in full (all of which can be found at the *Joseph Smith Papers* website and in Appendix B of this book) and can also evaluate for themselves the accuracy of the secondhand accounts. Anyone who reads the firsthand accounts in the Prophet's own words will be richly rewarded.

It is my hope that this book will help raise our appreciation for the First Vision, will provide opportunity for the Spirit to strengthen our testimonies of that vision, and will increase our ability to share and bear testimony of it ourselves. I am grateful that the Father and the Son condescended to visit Joseph Smith, and for all those who worked so hard to record or make available the accounts of this glorious event.

Chapter One

SEEKING

◆ Joseph Smith did not walk into a grove of trees one day and pray on a whim. He did not receive the most remarkable vision in this or perhaps any dispensation without preparation. A long series of events shaped who he was and why he would want to go to a grove to ask wisdom of God. If we want to seek God earnestly ourselves, we can do so better by learning what made Joseph Smith such an impassioned seeker.

Joseph Smith Sr.'s family faced hard times, brought on both by long and difficult winters and seasons, when their crops did not grow as they hoped, and by the dishonesty of partners they had involved themselves with. After some time, they found themselves nearly destitute, struggling to get by. Eventually they had to start over. In the winter of 1816–17, they moved to an area between the small towns of Manchester and Palmyra, New York. In the words of

Joseph's brother William, their circumstances "made an imperative demand upon every energy, nerve, or member of the family for both economy and labor, which this demand had to be met with the strictest kind of industry."[1] They tried to support themselves by making and selling barrels, candles, brooms, and baskets, and also by farming, selling baked goods, tapping maple trees, and working for others. In other words, they did whatever they could think of to try to get by and maybe even get ahead. These were hard times, and the whole family had to pitch in. It was a big family (ten people at the time), so it required a lot of work to take care of everyone. Joseph said that his father was "obliged to labor hard for the support of a large family."[2] Joseph had two older brothers, the eldest being almost eight years older than he was, and one older sister, who was two and a half years older. He had three younger brothers and a younger sister. Besides these siblings, an older and a younger brother had died as infants, and a younger sister would be born after Joseph prayed in the Sacred Grove. At the time of Joseph's vision, his youngest sibling was a brother who was eleven years younger than Joseph.

Joseph and his brothers and sisters worked hard for the family. They were not able to attend school often, because it took all their time and energy to contribute to

1. William Smith, "Notes on *Chamber's Encyclopedia*," as in Richard Lloyd Anderson, "Joseph Smith's Home Environment," *Ensign*, July 1971.
2. 1832 account.

the family's resources. Joseph Smith Sr. was fairly well educated and had once been a teacher. He could have provided some educational help for his children, but for the most part the family was not able to go to school the way they might have preferred. Furthermore, Joseph Sr. was so busy working that he could not spend as much of his time teaching his children as he surely would have liked. The financial struggles of his family weighed heavily on him.[3] He loved his children, and it must have dismayed him that instead of helping them get ahead by providing an inheritance for them, as his parents had done for him, he was instead requiring them to work so much that their education was lacking while their inheritance was not growing.[4]

Young Joseph worked hard to help support his family, and he looked up to his older brothers, Alvin and Hyrum, in how much work they were able to do. In his younger

---

3. For more information on the Smiths' financial difficulties and their impact on the family, see Richard Lyman Bushman, *Rough Stone Rolling* (New York: Alfred A. Knopf, 2006), 18–32; Steven C. Harper, *Joseph Smith's First Vision: A Guide to the Historical Accounts* (Salt Lake City: Deseret Book, 2012), 17–21; *Saints, The Story of the Church of Jesus Christ of Latter-day Saints, Volume 1: The Standard of Truth* (Salt Lake City: The Church of Jesus Christ of Latter-day Saints, 2018), 9–12; and Ivan J. Barrett, *Joseph Smith and the Restoration: A History of the Church to 1846* (Provo: Brigham Young University Press, 1974), 41–43.

4. When Joseph Smith Sr. gave Hyrum a patriarchal blessing on December 9, 1834, he spoke in what appears to be tones of regret about how Hyrum had borne the burden of supporting the family, and had "toiled hard and labored much" for the family, and had "stood by [his] father, and reached forth the helping hand to lift him up when he was in affliction."

years, Joseph was sometimes hampered in how much he could help because of an operation he'd had on the bones of his leg when he was quite young. This operation caused him to walk with a limp for many years and affected some of his abilities. Still, he eventually became known as a strong and hardworking young man.

During this time, the area where the Smith family lived experienced a great deal of interest in religion. The Methodists began preaching and reaching out to the people of the area, attempting to get them more excited about religion and to persuade them to join the Methodist Church.[5] Soon preachers from many churches came to the area, especially around Manchester, and held revival meetings. Baptists, Methodists, and Presbyterians each stirred up religious fervor, trying to encourage people to unite with their respective congregations.[6] People all around got caught up in the movement and tried to win others over to their point of view. Because the surrounding countryside was a farming community, most of the big revival meetings took place when there was not much happening in the way of farming, when preachers could get big turnouts. When it was planting or harvesting time, they knew the families, especially the men, would not be able to spare time for meetings. They did find ways to

5. In the 1838 account, Joseph Smith says that the Methodists began the excitement about religion in the area where he lived, and that it then spread to other sects.

6. 1842 account.

reach out to families, especially women, during the farming season, but the big religious pushes came during the off-season.

Joseph's family got caught up in the religious movement. Like everyone around them, they fervently wanted to be saved. But Joseph found himself caught between the two very different religious approaches of his parents.[7] His mother had nearly died years earlier, and as part of that experience had promised God she would diligently search for the religion that would help her serve God correctly.[8] She was convinced that the organized churches all around them were part of the process of salvation. She wanted her family to choose a church and be faithful to it. At the time, America was experiencing a religious split that was also manifest in the Smith family. Calvinist-leaning churches, such as the Presbyterians, felt that humanity was depraved and that Christ had atoned for the sins of only a few who would be saved.[9] Others, such as the Methodists, believed mankind was fallen but not depraved, and that Christ would save all those who

---

7. In the 1832 account, Joseph Smith says that his parents "spared no pains in instructing me in the christian religion." Thus we can assume that he knew quite a bit about each of his parents' religious views.

8. Harper, *Joseph Smith's First Vision*, 18.

9. Harper, *Joseph Smith's First Vision*, 15; and Jonathan Edwards, "Sinners in the Hands of an Angry God," in John E. Smith, Harry S. Stout, and Kenneth P. Minkema, eds., *A Jonathan Edwards Reader* (New Haven: Yale University Press, 2003), 96.

chose to follow Him.[10] Joseph's mother, Lucy, his brothers Hyrum and Samuel, and his sister Sophronia all joined the Presbyterian Church.[11]

In contrast, Joseph Smith Sr. felt that all churches had good elements to them but that they were not necessary for coming to Christ and being saved. To him it was more important to approach God and less important to do it in the way that someone else prescribed. Some of these feelings probably came from dreams he had experienced. Joseph Smith Sr. had been blessed with several dreams he felt were from God that convinced him that the religions around him were lacking and that he personally was still missing something in order to receive exaltation.[12] Additionally, he was likely looking for more information to come from a relative, because his father had said that "it has been borne in upon my soul that one of my descendants will promulgate a work to revolutionize the world of religious faith."[13] Expecting this event probably made Joseph Smith Sr. somewhat mistrust the religious organizations around him since he knew someone would bring forth something new from God. He likely assumed that each religion was missing something important and that he should just love God and serve Him while waiting for the

10. Harper, *Joseph Smith's First Vision*, 14–15.

11. 1838 account.

12. Lucy Mack Smith, *Biographical Sketches of Joseph Smith* (Liverpool: S. W. Richards, 1853), 74; and Barrett, *Joseph Smith and the Restoration*, 35.

13. Barrett, *Joseph Smith and the Restoration*, 22.

promise to be fulfilled. Joseph Smith Sr., his father, and two of his brothers had helped form a Universalist society that espoused just this kind of thinking. As a result of all this, Joseph's mother wanted him to join any church to be saved, and his father felt it best to not join the wrong church but instead to serve and love God. Thus, even at home, young Joseph could not find an answer as to what he should do about joining churches and how he could be saved.

For years these questions weighed upon Joseph's mind.[14] He became convinced that without help from on high, his soul would be damned. As Joseph described it, "My mind become exceedingly distressed for I become convicted of my sins," and "I felt to mourn for my own sins and for the sins of the world."[15] He desperately wanted to be saved and did not want to take a chance that he was relying on the wrong idea of how to receive salvation.[16] Joseph went to meetings with his family[17] and saw them and others "get religion." Usually this meant that they were touched by the Spirit and would stand up and let those around them know they loved Jesus, were saved by Him, and would

---

14. In the 1832 account, Joseph Smith notes that he was about twelve when "[his] mind become seriously imprest with regard to the all important concerns for the well fare of [his] immortal Soul." He then notes that this was a concern of his from the age of twelve to fifteen. While Joseph seems to have been searching for the exact ages he was during all of this, it is clear that it lasted for several years.

15. 1832 account.

16. 1840 Orson Pratt account.

17. 1838 account.

follow Him. Typically those who experienced these feelings joined whatever church they were in when they had that experience, and often baptism followed. While most people were probably sincere and had truly felt a spiritual sensation that caused them to be full of a love of God and a zeal for serving Him, we can safely assume that some people saw others around them having these experiences and, not wanting their family or neighbors to think there was something wrong with them, they pretended to "get religion." It may have been a small portion, but undoubtedly some people manifested a religious experience they had not felt just so others would not look down on them.

It is remarkable that young Joseph, even at the age of twelve or thirteen, would not fabricate religious experiences. He was too sincere, too full of integrity. He desperately wanted to have the Spirit manifest to him. He wanted to "get religion" and know that he was doing things the right way and with the right church. But Joseph did not have those feelings come to him, and he was not going to pretend that he had. This matter was too important to him. His mother and some of his siblings felt moved, and they stood and shouted their convictions. As much as Joseph wanted to join them, and as much as he must have worried about what they thought of him, he just wasn't feeling the Spirit when they were, so he could not make himself join them in their exuberant religious experiences. He later said that he "wanted to feel and shout like the rest but he could feel nothing."[18] Despite describing being caught up in the excitement of the religious revivals and wanting desperately to enjoy the exuberance of salvation, young Joseph remained true to the feelings he was actually experiencing.

It made no sense to teenage Joseph that so many churches would claim to be Christ's when they did not agree on a great many important issues.[19] He struggled with the idea that joining any of them would be fine, which is what part of his family seemed to believe. How could it be right to join whatever church struck your fancy when they differed on so many important points of doctrine?[20] Yet Joseph also struggled with his father's idea that it wasn't important to align with any religion. The truth about salvation must exist, he reasoned, and if so, then he needed to find out who had the truth and how he could know it.[21] Taking in both some of his mother's ideas and some of his father's, Joseph found himself in an almost impossible situation. He believed he needed to join a church, but he did not want to join the wrong one, and no matter how hard he tried, he just couldn't figure out which one was right.[22]

18. Alexander Neibaur, in his 1843 journal account, says that Joseph's mother, brother, and sister "got religion" and that Joseph wanted to get religion and feel and shout too, but that he just didn't feel anything.

19. 1842 account.

20. 1842 account.

21. 1840 Orson Pratt account.

22. 1838 account.

Joseph was always prone to pondering and thinking about deep things. Everyone in his family read, but Joseph perused books less than the others. It seems that he developed the habit of contemplating at length about those things he heard and studied deeply. As his mother described, Joseph was "much less inclined to the perusal of books than any of the rest of our children, but far more given to meditation and deep study."[23] During those years of religious revival, Joseph took to studying the scriptures to try to find answers to his questions. He read and pondered again and again, for years, trying to figure out what he should do.[24] Joseph had been taught, and he fervently believed, that the Bible was the word of God[25] and that it contained the words of salvation. He knew he needed to be saved, and he hoped that studying the scriptures would tell him exactly how to obtain salvation and which group could best help him do so. He began to silently pray[26] as part of his pondering. He also continued to read the Bible.

23. Lucy Mack Smith, *History of Joseph Smith by His Mother, Lucy Mack Smith* (Salt Lake City: Bookcraft, 1979), 82.

24. The idea that he did this for years is based on the 1832 account, which says that he started thinking about these things at about the age of twelve.

25. In the 1832 account, Joseph Smith says that he searched the scriptures, having been taught that they contained the word of God.

26. It is clear that Joseph's prayer in the grove was not his first prayer about this matter. The 1842 Orson Hyde account mentions that he prayed about this often and eventually went to the grove to pray. Yet in the 1838 account he says it was his first vocal attempt at prayer. Thus we can assume that he had prayed silently about it beforehand.

As Joseph studied the scriptures, he became more concerned. The more familiar he was with the word of God and the more he went to meetings in different churches, the more he became convinced that many of their teachings and behaviors did not measure up to what he was learning in the Bible.[27] This was especially true in how they treated each other when it came to contesting for converts. It seemed to him that their sermons on love quickly turned to expressions of anger, contention, and hatred if they saw potential converts joining another church. This distressed Joseph, constituting what he called "a grief to my soul,"[28] which caused him "extreme difficulties."[29] Though there was one Methodist minister Joseph respected and trusted more than the others,[30] Joseph was agitated, feeling that he needed to be saved, looking for someone to guide him, wanting to trust religious leaders to teach him, but not seeing them square themselves to the Bible the way he thought they should.

27. In the 1832 account, Joseph Smith says that he discovered that the churches did not adorn themselves by a holy walk and holy conversation agreeable to what he read in the scriptures.

28. Quote from the 1832 account. In the 1838 account, Joseph Smith speaks of the contention for converts by the ministers and priests and how it went against the things they were teaching. The 1842 Orson Hyde account speaks of the denominations being poisoned by hate, contention, resentment, and anger.

29. 1838 account.

30. See Larry C. Porter, "Reverend George Lane—Good 'Gifts,' Much 'Grace,' Marked 'Usefulness,'" *BYU Studies* 9:3 (Spring 1969), 328; see also Harper, *Joseph Smith's First Vision*, 24–26.

He pondered the contentions and wickedness of the world, as well as the contention between religious denominations, and he felt saddened and lost. He also feared for the welfare of his own soul, since he could not find the answers he was searching for in any of the churches around him.[31] He began to fear that he would be damned. Eternal consequences were on the line, and Joseph was desperate to find the right answer, "considering it to be of the first importance that I should be right, in matters that involved eternal consequences."[32]

Part of the difficulty lay in Joseph's youth. As a young teenager, he did not feel he fully understood all the vehement arguments between the religious groups he visited.[33] He did not feel experienced enough to see through smooth and eloquent opinions, and he could find no one to rely on. His family had different opinions, his neighbors had different opinions, and he did not trust his ability to see his way through the thicket of ideas bombarding him.[34] He was starting to lean toward becoming a Methodist, but he was not sure of himself enough to commit to that group when there were so many contradicting arguments and so much was at stake.[35]

---

31. 1840 Orson Pratt account.

32. 1835 account; spelling standardized.

33. 1838 account.

34. 1840 Orson Pratt account.

35. The 1842 Orson Hyde account speaks of Joseph's fear of not learning the proper path and his hesitancy to leave finding that path up to chance.

During all this commotion, the family moved into a log cabin on some land they were renting and farming with an agreement that their rent payments could go toward buying the land. Thus the Smith family found themselves caught up in great concern for their spiritual lives at the same time they were concerned for their physical lives. Each family member had to give her or his all to move and to create a farm that could sustain the entire family. Between visiting religious groups and leaders, sifting through religious thoughts, moving, farming, working for others, clearing more land for farming, and searching and pondering the scriptures, Joseph Smith must have had a busy time during the winter and early spring of 1820. It was also a time of anxiety. Despite his strong desire to learn how to be saved, and despite all his earnest efforts, he still hadn't figured out what to do.

Chapter Two

———————◆———————

ASKING

꧁ The spring of 1820 was a good time for the Smith family. The weather was better than it had been during the years that had devastated their crops. The older boys were big enough to be a real help on the family farm and could also work for others and bring home some money. They were clearing more and more of the land they were renting, cutting down trees so they could plant more crops.[1] Even the youngest child was now turning four years old and would likely be able to do some simple chores to contribute. Life was beginning to look better.

As bright as all of this must have looked to Joseph Jr., he had not yet been able to find a salve for his worried soul. During the winter months when no farming could be done, he would have been able to find more time to attend religious meetings and study the Bible. This had

1. Bushman, *Rough Stone Rolling*, 32–33.

only brought him more confusion, however, and not the answers he was hoping for. He was not able to "satisfy the anxious desires that pervaded his breast."[2] He was an unusually perceptive youth,[3] with an ability to see core issues: Why didn't the churches agree with each other? Why didn't any of them seem to match with what he was reading in scripture? Was salvation limited or abundantly available? How was salvation available, and what must be done to receive it? His ability to recognize these issues and to form questions about them actually led to more confusion, not less, since his attempts to answer these questions only highlighted the inability of the churches around him to do so.[4] He could plainly see how the most important issues were tied up with the ability to receive salvation, and fully realized how important it was to find answers to the questions surrounding those issues. The problem was that there seemed to be no answers to these core questions. Though he continued to lean toward Methodism, there were too many contradictions, too many arguments, too many sophisticated and convincing sermons that were at odds with others that were equally appealing and suave.[5] Moreover, the questions were too important; too much was on the line.

---

2. 1840 Orson Pratt account.

3. 1842 Orson Hyde account.

4. 1842 Orson Hyde account.

5. 1838 account.

In particular and as noted above, the Methodism of Joseph's day, which taught of a universally available salvation, was in conflict with the Calvinist ideas of Presbyterianism, which taught that only some could be saved. Some of his father's ideas, which were somewhat expressed in Methodism, seem to have been attractive to young Joseph. At the same time, the precepts of his mother's Presbyterian faith probably nagged at the back of his mind, telling him he needed to know for sure whether he was saved or not, in case it was true that only some people would be saved. After yet another winter of earnest preachers and revival meetings, these same competing ideas had created no solution in Joseph's uneasy mind.

This was a heavy and disturbing scenario for a boy who was just over fourteen years old. Still, the work of the family and the farm had to press on. As the winter turned to spring and agricultural efforts would have taken precedence over time for revival meetings, Joseph must have often found himself with time to ask deep questions and contemplate the things of God only as he worked on the farm. Fortunately, that kind of work lends itself to opportunities for deep thought.

Joseph was convinced that one of the churches must be the right one. He believed that God was not the author of confusion; while the differing opinions could not all be of God, *one* of them had to be, he reasoned.[6] His

---

6. 1840 Orson Pratt account.

desire and efforts became concentrated less on having the kind of spiritual revival experience that others were having and more on figuring out which church was from God. He turned his pondering and searching upon this question: Which church practiced the doctrines of God the way God intended; which church was God's?[7]

Although Joseph had been praying and searching the scriptures for a while by this point,[8] he was losing confidence in being able to use the Bible to determine which church was correct because he heard different ministers interpret the same scriptures so differently.[9] He thought that a passage of scripture told him something about how Christ's church should look or operate, but then he would hear a minister interpret the same passage very differently. Thus he grew increasingly unconfident in his ability to use the Bible to determine which church was God's.[10] Still he seemed to think that some kind of guidance could come through his scripture study, and he maintained confidence that he could be guided to answers while studying the Bible.[11] He continued searching it, probably also hoping that while studying the scriptures he could experience the kind of spiritual rebirth he saw others have in meetings.

It is significant to realize that it was the lack of answers

7. 1840 Orson Pratt account.

8. 1840 Orson Pratt account.

9. 1842 Orson Hyde account.

10. 1838 account and 1842 Orson Hyde account.

11. 1842 Orson Hyde account.

that drove Joseph to ask the Lord. Speaking of what eventually led him to the Sacred Grove, he later recalled, "I cried unto the Lord for mercy, for there was none else to whom I could go."[12] The answers coming from the world around him were failing him. He was coming to realize that only God could answer his questions.

One day, Joseph spent time cutting down trees on a part of the family's rented land some distance from the log cabin where they were living. This labor was part of the family effort to clear trees to create land on which they could plant crops. As the day wound down and time for dinner drew nigh, Joseph thrust his ax deep into the stump of a tree he had cut down, presumably intending to return in the morning to begin work again, and started walking back home for dinner.[13] Having worked so much that day, he must have had a lot of time to think through the important questions of salvation that had been plaguing him, and we can assume he thought on the subject as he walked home too.[14]

Sometime after dinner he must have wanted to search for answers once again. As was Joseph's wont, he turned to the scriptures, hoping to find some clue as to which

---

12. 1832 account.

13. 1843 interview.

14. While a teenage boy will think about many things when given time for pondering, the events of that night and the next day cause me to assume that on this day, Joseph Smith's thoughts were more drawn to religious questions than usual.

church was teaching the truth. It seems that he was not reading through the Bible systematically, but was instead reading first in one spot, then in another.[15] On this night he turned to the Epistle of James. Joseph had heard a minister read a passage from the first chapter that had seemed meaningful to him, so Joseph turned to read and ponder it for himself.[16] He had not been reading from James for long before he had an intense religious experience like he had never had before, despite longing to have one for some time. In the passage in question, the fifth verse of the first chapter, he read, "If any of you lack wisdom, let him ask of God, that giveth to all men liberally, and upbraideth not; and it shall be given him." When Joseph read this verse, the Holy Ghost carried it deeply into his heart, searing in both his mind and his feelings that this was exactly what he needed to do. In his own words, "Never did any passage of scripture come with more power to the heart of man than this did at this time

15. In the 1843 interview, Joseph Smith says he opened the Bible "promiscuously" to James. I take this to mean that he opened it somewhat randomly, though that is difficult to square with the account that he had heard James read earlier in the day, which made him want to read it again. Thus it seems most likely to me that he had not been reading the Bible through by course, but rather read what fancied him at the moment, and that hearing James earlier in the day caused him to turn to that passage as his reading.

16. "Statement of William Smith, Concerning Joseph, the Prophet," *Deseret Evening News*, 20 January 1894, 11. See also Harper, *Joseph Smith's First Vision*, 25; *Saints*, vol. 1, 13.

to mine. It seemed to enter with great force into every feeling of my heart" (Joseph Smith—History 1:12).[17] The power of that experience seemed to affect every thought and feeling Joseph had. He could not stop thinking about it. Again and again he pondered the meaning of the verse and the feelings of "great joy" that had overcome him as he'd read it.[18] As he pondered, he also remembered other scriptures that explained that he who asked would receive, to him that knocked the door would be opened, and he that sought would find (see Matthew 7:7–8).[19]

These scriptures all suggested there was another way for Joseph to get his answers. He had tried learning from his family about the path to salvation, but he had gotten mixed messages. He had turned to ministers and religious people who lived in his area, but they also had given him conflicting opinions. Because the ministers had interpreted the scriptures he read in such varying ways, he was losing hope in learning the truth from the written word of God. But now those scriptures had given Joseph the idea that he could bypass everything and everyone else and find out from God Himself what God would have Joseph do. What a liberating thought! Perhaps Joseph really could find out how to be saved, for it seemed as

---

17. 1838 account.

18. 1840 Orson Hyde account.

19. In the 1835 account, Joseph Smith quotes and paraphrases these verses, though he does not provide the citation for them.

if God would be willing to tell him personally. Joseph felt this verse was like a beam of "light shining forth in a dark place, to guide him to the path in which he should walk."[20] For the first time in a long time he could see the way to go, or at least the way to learn how to press on.

We can more fully understand the way the Spirit must have moved the nascent prophet that night if we recall all that he had already done by the time he read from the Bible that fateful evening. It was not as if Joseph hadn't already spent a long time searching the scriptures and seeking for truth there as well as from family, friends, and ministers. It wasn't as if he had never prayed and sought guidance in this important matter. It wasn't as if he hadn't spent years pondering and puzzling over these things. At this point in the story it is overly apparent that Joseph had paid his dues in seeking for answers. Yet as he read from James that night, apparently something different happened. It was time, and the Spirit seems to have moved upon him in such a powerful way that he knew there was something different about this experience. The Spirit seemingly led him to believe that it was time for him to make a serious effort at vocal prayer, earnestly asking God which church had the answers he needed and the ability to guide him toward salvation. The Holy Ghost seems to have also moved him so powerfully that Joseph became

20. 1840 Orson Pratt account.

sure that this time he would get an answer.[21] He fully believed what James had said and was ready to put it into action. He knew that he could remain in a feeling of frustration, anxiety, and darkness forever, or he could go ask God for direction, with a certainty that it would come.[22] But he could not have known the power of the answer he would receive, nor what that answer would be.

The next morning was beautiful, bright, and clear.[23] Joseph awoke with a determination to put his plan into action. He went back to the clearing where he had been working, the place he had left his ax the night before.[24] There he found not only the clearing they had been creating but also, just a little further past it, a place where he was surrounded by trees, out of sight and earshot of others—a place he could be alone with his thoughts and his prayers and God. Though in that grove there may have been birds singing, being surrounded by trees also created a feeling of privacy, and the trees absorbed other sounds. To Joseph, at least, it was quiet. It was peaceful. He looked around and was sure he was alone.[25] He was

---

21. 1842 Orson Hyde account.

22. In the 1835 account, Joseph Smith says that in order to escape confusion he knew he needed information from God, and so he went to the grove with a fixed determination to obtain it.

23. 1838 account.

24. 1843 interview.

25. 1838 account.

ready to offer his first vocal prayer to ask God which church held the path to salvation.

Yet the peace did not remain. As Joseph opened his mouth to pray, asking, "Oh Lord, what church should I join?"[26] other forces began to move against him. At first he thought he heard noises behind him, as if someone were sneaking up on him. He looked but could see no one. He tried praying again. He again heard noises, and he felt sure that someone was walking toward him. He stopped, jumped up, and looked around. He could not find anyone anywhere near.[27] He began to feel startled and afraid, not knowing why he would hear such sounds yet not see anyone. He felt the doubts and fear that accompany being startled, feelings that make it difficult to feel faith and hope. Still, he was determined to pray and was not going to allow anything to stop him.

Joseph redoubled his efforts but found another obstacle being imposed upon him. As he began again to try praying aloud, he found his tongue felt swollen, and it seemed to stick in his mouth.[28] He tried and tried, but he

26. In the 1843 interview, it appears that this was the question he began his prayer with, even before he was beset upon by Satan.

27. In the 1835 account, Joseph Smith says that as he prayed he heard "a noise behind me like some person walking towards me." He then tried to pray again, but could not, presumably because of the swollen tongue he mentions in this account. Then he heard the noise of walking drawing nearer, which caused him to spring to his feet, but he could not see anyone that would make the noise he was hearing.

28. 1835 account.

could not make his mouth work nor separate his tongue from the roof of his mouth.[29] Feelings of darkness filled his heart and mind, making him feel as if he were "doomed to sudden destruction" (Joseph Smith—History 1:15). This was more than the fear that accompanies being startled; this was a fear imposed upon him by an outside source. Joseph was overcome with doubt.[30] The feeling of shadow increased, growing stronger and stronger,[31] and his mind was filled with images of fear,[32] probably compounded by the experience of thinking he had heard someone, or something, creeping up behind him, but not solely from that experience.

Soon Joseph began to realize that this was not just a dark feeling. While the overpowering gloom was real and the feelings of despair were inescapable, he came to realize that there was a being behind that feeling. He soon understood that he was under a real attack, and that a being whom he could not see was assaulting him.[33] This

---

29. 1844 Alexander Neibaur account.

30. 1842 Orson Hyde account.

31. The 1840 Orson Pratt account speaks of Joseph Smith being severely tempted by the powers of darkness that endeavored to overcome him.

32. The 1842 Orson Hyde account says that besides being bombarded with doubt, Joseph's mind was filled with all manner of inappropriate images. In our day, the phrase "inappropriate images" carries connotations that it would not have in the era of Orson Hyde. The most likely conclusion is that images of fear and things that could happen to him were what bombarded Joseph Smith.

33. 1838 account.

being had immense power and was full of darkness and desolation. Joseph felt himself sinking and began to lose hope that he would survive.[34] He did not seem to be able to talk. He was starting to lose the ability to even think. He was beginning to believe that he would not make it through the attack, that the being who was assaulting him was too powerful and too malevolent.[35]

The boy-turning-prophet was learning firsthand that one of Satan's greatest tools is a black feeling of despair. Despair rips into hope and faith and eats away at the desire to approach God. Feelings of despair can come from many sources and in many ways, but if they remain for any length of time, they always tear away at the foundations of love, hope, and faith that lead toward God. They often seem to mute the ability to feel the Spirit. This is a tool Satan delights in employing, and it was the main weapon from his arsenal that he aimed at Joseph Smith at this crucial juncture. He unleashed upon the boy prophet an unrelenting wave of dark feelings, attempting to crush Joseph's young spirit beneath the burden of hopelessness, doubt, and fear. Though Joseph and his family had been through tough times, his temperament was naturally cheery and optimistic.[36] He therefore would have been unaccustomed to feelings of darkness, much less to the

34. 1838 account.

35. 1838 account.

36. 1838 account.

crushing weight of woe and shadow that the devil himself attempted to smother Joseph with. This was an attack from a being of immense power and immeasurable experience. Moreover, this being was overfamiliar with feelings of despair and knew how to wield them powerfully. It was more than the boy would be able to withstand on his own, for none of us can resist an unfettered Satan by relying solely upon our own powers. How much less was an innocent fourteen-year-old farm boy prepared to withstand such an onslaught on his own? [37]

Joseph was beginning to fear that there was no way to endure this assault. Yet he was determined to try, and he kept attempting to pray. He must have continued to pray within his heart, but he also kept trying to pray aloud. [38] Though he pushed forward in prayer, he was on the verge of abandoning all hope when he felt some degree of relief. It was as if another merciful power gave him just enough strength to survive, to continue to push forward in prayer. [39] And so he prayed, feeling as if his life depended on it, and with just an inkling of hope forming within. [40] As he continued to pray his tongue was loosed,

---

37. See the account of Satan attacking Moses in Moses 1:12–22. A mature Moses was not able to rid himself of Satan until he invoked the power of God.

38. 1838 account.

39. 1842 Orson Hyde account.

40. The 1840 Orson Pratt account speaks of Joseph continuing to seek for deliverance and eventually finding enough release from darkness that we was enabled to pray again. The 1842 Orson Hyde account

30

and he found his mouth delivered so that he could pray out loud again.[41] He pled for deliverance, and deliverance came. It first took the form of light.

At the unexpected and sudden appearance of a blazing burst of light, the darkness fled. "Light and darkness cannot occupy the same space at the same time. Light dispels darkness. When light is present, darkness is vanquished and must depart."[42] There is no doubt that Satan desired to control Joseph Smith and to sift him as wheat (see Luke 22:31). But as God has promised so often, prayer is what gives us power to withstand Satan and come off conqueror rather than be conquered (see D&C 10:5). Joseph Smith found this to be true and saw first-hand that the blackness of the prince of darkness cannot withstand the burning light of the Son of God. In Joseph's own words, as the light came, "I was filled with the Spirit of God, and the Lord opened the heavens upon me."[43] Joseph knew he had been delivered by a holy and pure power that was well beyond him. He had been rescued by the power of God.

---

relates that the mercy of God allowed him to keep praying and that after this small deliverance he kept praying and then light and peace filled his heart, which enabled him to try praying again. These details seem specific and reliable, but we cannot be sure of their accuracy.

41. In the 1835 account, Joseph Smith says eventually, "My mouth was opened and my toung liberated."

42. Robert D. Hales, "Out of Darkness into His Marvelous Light," *Ensign*, May 2002.

43. 1832 account, punctuation standardized.

Chapter Three

FINDING

Joseph's escape from darkness brought with it a great sense of relief. The horrifying weight fled, and the sense of dread and loss of hope went with it. The relief was real and palpable, for it filled Joseph "with joy unspeakable."[1] Yet the exit of a dark, hopeless fear did not mean that all Joseph's concern was gone. Instead, the fear was replaced by a strange mixture of joy, hope, and worry.

Joseph saw in the sky far above him such a blaze of light that he didn't know how to describe it. In later years he alternately compared it to the light of fire or of the sun,[2] the two greatest sources of light he had ever

---

1. 1835 account.

2. The 1832 account records the word "fire," which was crossed out and followed by the word "light." The 1835 account describes a "pillar of fire." The 1838 account describes light "above the brightness of the sun." The 1842 account speaks of a light that "eclipsed the sun at noon-day." Only one of the secondhand accounts makes a comparison

experienced. He said it was brighter than either. The light started far above him and slowly descended toward him.[3] It was unlike anything he had seen or felt before. It was, literally, unworldly. It was so different from anything he had experienced that throughout his life he found himself unable to fully describe it to others.

As the light descended from on high it grew more dazzling and broader.[4] It began to spread out, illuminating the forested area where Joseph was.[5] At the same time, it grew brighter and brighter.[6] Joseph felt as if it was so bright it could eclipse the noonday sun.[7] Soon it seemed to him that the land for some distance around was bathed in this incredible light.[8] It was the appearance of that light that had delivered him, and he knew it.[9] With the light had come a great sense of hope and comforting peace.[10]

---

to either fire or the sun, and that is the latest account, by Alexander Neibaur. In that account, Neibaur recalls the prophet saying that "he saw a fire towards heaven."

3. 1840 Orson Pratt account; 1844 Alexander Naibaur account.

4. 1840 Orson Pratt account.

5. 1840 Orson Pratt account.

6. 1840 Orson Pratt account.

7. 1838 account.

8. 1840 Orson Pratt account.

9. 1838 account.

10. Alexander Neibaur's 1844 account speaks of a feeling of comfort coming as the fire enveloped Joseph. This is a secondhand account and so the differing order cannot be fully relied upon. Thus, while the Neibaur account makes sense based on the order of feelings presented below, we cannot fully trust it.

Yet the light was so strong and was growing so much that it seemed to Joseph that when it touched the trees where he stood, they would surely burst into flame. The light was that bright, that powerful; it seemed unthinkable that the trees would not burn. How could he survive such a raging fire? There was a part of Joseph that feared that having been delivered from the darkness, he would be consumed by the light.[11] How ironic that must have seemed.

When we read the accounts of people who have had heavenly visions, they always seem to struggle with finding language to describe their experiences. We also often see that their experiences with beings and power so much higher than our own plane of existence caused them to fear. The glory of God and His messengers is awe-inspiring in the true meaning of the word. They are awe-ful, meaning that they are so wonderful they become frightening, and thus they can evoke terror, or seem terrible. Again and again in the scriptures we find that those who see God are overawed, and we see heavenly beings usually have to begin their discourse with mortals by first telling them that there is no need to fear. Beholding such a presence seems to naturally inspire a certain kind of fear.

Joseph Smith Jr. felt a degree of fear as he watched the brilliant, powerful light of heaven coming ever closer to him. Yet this worry was short-lived. He was amazed, like Moses, when he saw the light first shine from above,

11. 1840 Orson Pratt account.

then rest upon the trees so brightly that it looked as if they were on fire, yet they did not burn.[12] There was light, but no flame. When he saw that the trees did not burst into flames as they were touched by the light, Joseph was greatly encouraged, for it seemed, then, that he might survive as well.[13]

Eventually the light rested upon Joseph himself. When the light did touch him, it brought with it not a searing heat but instead a powerful and unparalleled sensation.[14] He was immediately filled with a sense of peace and joy that he had never known before, even "joy unspeakable."[15] This was a feeling that was beyond his capacity to experience on his own. He was fully engulfed in a sensation he could only describe as the "spirit of God."[16]

It is likely that at least some of what Joseph was experiencing was the sanctifying power of God, bringing about what we call transfiguration, for all who come into God's presence need to be transfigured. In his fallen state, Joseph would have had good reason to fear; he would not have survived an encounter with God. Joseph was about to come into the presence of God the Father Himself, a being whose purity and glory were beyond Joseph's

---

12. In the 1835 account, Joseph Smith says that "this pillar of flame was spread all around, and yet nothing consumed."

13. 1840 Orson Pratt account.

14. 1840 Orson Pratt account.

15. 1835 account.

16. 1832 account.

ability to withstand. Yet with God all things are possible, and Joseph's nature was temporarily changed to a higher state. This is what happened to Moses when he experienced God's presence (see Moses 1:2). It would seem, then, that at least part of the sensation the young prophet experienced as the light fell upon him was the feeling of being transfigured. Becoming a being of a higher realm, even if only temporarily, must have changed him for that time into a being that felt greater love, joy, and peace. Joseph was catching just a glimpse of what it felt to be Christlike. He was becoming, for a moment, a being that was compatible with the presence of a celestial being. This must have been a "peculiar sensation" indeed.[17]

There was another effect that came over Joseph when the light fell upon him. There was no doubt that what was happening was taking place in the world. Joseph saw the light resting on the trees near him and illuminating the wilderness all around, so the event had to have been taking place in the real world, in the actual geographic location where the young man was. Yet he reported that when the light rested upon him he found himself "enwrapped in a heavenly vision," and that he no longer saw the world around him.[18]

---

17. In the 1840 Orson Pratt account, Pratt says that as the light came upon him, Joseph Smith experienced a "peculiar sensation."

18. 1838 account. This is also in the 1840 Orson Pratt account. In the 1842 Orson Hyde account, it says that the "world around him was excluded from his view," making it sound as if the most likely scenario is

Other prophets have also testified that when they saw visions they could not tell if they were happening in the place where their body was or if they were caught away to somewhere else (see, for example, 2 Corinthians 12:2). Joseph could have been caught up to another place. But the wording also suggests the possibility that as the light rested upon him and he began to see the things of God and the heavenly world, he was so focused on those things that he no longer saw or noticed the things of this world.

Though we have just gone through it in great detail, it is worth trying to retrace in a simpler way the progress of Joseph's deliverance and the feelings that seem to have accompanied it, based on the sources cited above.

- At the height of the darkness overcoming the prophet's heart and mind, as Joseph was about to give up, he seems to have been given just enough feeling of hope and encouragement to keep praying.
- As he kept praying, he saw a light.
- The appearance of the light chased the dark feelings from him and seems to have brought a greater sense of relief, hope, peace, and joy.
- Those feelings were quickly intermingled with feelings of worry about the potential for the woods around him to burst into flames.
- We can presume that this worry dissipated when the

that he was so focused on the heavenly things he saw that he no longer noticed the earthly which was around him.

trees remained intact. It is reported that he was encouraged by seeing that they did not burn.

♦ It seems that the strongest sensation occurred when the light rested upon Joseph himself. This seems to be when he experienced such a feeling of joy that he could not describe it.[19]

♦ It also appears that this was accompanied by a "peculiar" sensation, which was likely the effect of transfiguration. As noted above, such transfiguration probably increased Joseph's ability to feel joy, peace, and love, which are all fruits of the Spirit, which he was certainly being infused with.

♦ In the midst of all this great wash of feelings and sensations, Joseph became unaware of the world around him. In so many ways he was having an experience that went beyond this world.

As the things of this world faded from Joseph's mind, that which he saw was so glorious that he could never describe it. As he looked into the pillar of light, he saw a being descend until it stood just above him, not quite touching the ground.[20] This was God the Father, whom very, very few have seen since the Fall.[21] As recalled by one convert, Joseph described Him as wearing white

---

19. 1835 account.

20. The 1835 account mentions just one being. The 1838 account mentions that the beings Joseph saw did not touch the ground.

21. While the 1835 account mentions only one being, most speak of two. The 1843 interview mentions that They did not come at the same time, and that the first being introduced the second as His Son.

robes that covered His shoulder but left His right arm bare.[22] This same convert also remembered Joseph saying that the Father had blue eyes and a light complexion.[23]

We cannot imagine what it was like to be in the presence of a divine being so full of might and majesty. When Joseph spoke of this experience at different times, he used phrases such as "whose brightness and glory defy all description,"[24] or "glorious personage,"[25] or "glorious heavenly personages."[26]

As he looked at this being of might and majesty, Joseph did not yet know who the being was. Soon after seeing the Father, Joseph was able to see another being, one who came to stand at the side of the first.[27] This personage was also full of glory beyond description. In fact, the two who stood before the youth looked alike. Joseph said They "exactly resembled each other in features, and likeness"[28] or "in features and stature."[29] Apparently there

22. 1844 Alexander Neibaur account. Because this is a secondhand account, and is singular in recording these details, we cannot be certain of them. Yet they are worth including here for consideration. Typically such a specific detail is not misremembered or accidentally created in the mind of the listener.

23. 1844 Alexander Neibaur account.

24. 1838 account.

25. 1843 interview.

26. 1842 Orson Hyde account.

27. 1835 account.

28. 1838 account; also in the 1840 Orson Pratt account.

29. 1842 Orson Hyde account. Where Orson Pratt and Joseph Smith use the word "likeness," the Orson Hyde account says "stature." In this

was a very strong Father-Son resemblance between the two, which was probably enhanced by the fact that They were both so full of a bright glory that differed so much from the things of this world. In any case, Joseph now found himself looking at both the Father and the Son, two glorious personages standing in the air just close enough that They could touch him, bathed in the magnificent light of heaven. Joseph must have also been immersed in the feeling of love that must have emanated from Them.

After Joseph was able to see the Son, the Father, whose voice has so seldom been heard in this fallen world, spoke to Joseph. He pointed to the second being and said, "Joseph, this is My Beloved Son, hear Him!"[30] At last Joseph knew the identities of the beings that stood before him. Now he knew that he was in the presence of Deity, that he stood before God the Father and God the Son. And God had called Joseph by name! The Father knew him intimately and referred to him specifically.

After this the Son spoke. The first thing He said was, "Joseph, my son, thy sins are forgiven thee."[31] Oh, how much this statement must have meant to the boy who had

case it seems likely that Orson Hyde remembered and used a different word than that which Joseph Smith had used, but it is possible that the Prophet used different words at different times and Hyde remembered a different occasion than Pratt.

30. 1838 account.

31. 1832 account. In the 1835 account, Joseph Smith also notes that he was told his sins were forgiven, as does Orson Pratt in his 1840 account. It is not fully clear whether it was the Son or the Father who

gone to the grove. It is worth considering why it would have been so powerful. First, like the Father, Christ knew Joseph's name. Second, Christ called him "my son," a phrase filled with love, intimacy, and belonging. To hear the Savior call Joseph His son must have meant so much and been so endearing. Further, and perhaps most important for Joseph, he had been told that his sins were forgiven.

We must remember that the whole journey to the grove had begun with Joseph becoming "convicted" of his sins[32] and realizing that he needed forgiveness if he was ever to receive salvation and have the kind of life in the eternities that he wanted. It was concern for the welfare of his soul and knowledge of his sins that had brought Joseph to the grove in the first place. What comfort and joy it must have been for him to hear that his sins were forgiven! He must have been much more able to listen to everything else that God would tell him that day once this overarching burden was removed. Joseph Smith, at that moment, did not have to worry about his worthiness or his sinfulness. He was forgiven!

---

told Joseph that his sins were forgiven. See the footnote associated with the summary of the 1835 account in Appendix A.

32. 1832 account.

Chapter Four

LEARNING

After being told by the Savior that he was forgiven, testimony that Jesus was the Son of God was borne to Joseph.[1] Joseph was also told to go his way and walk in the Lord's statutes and commandments.[2] The Savior often forgives or commends; He also reminds of the need to do better. Joseph was forgiven, but it was clear that this did not mean his struggles with sin were over. He now knew with certainty that he could be forgiven. But he also knew that he would need to continue to focus on keeping the commands of God.

Joseph was then favored with another thing few in this world have been able to hear. The Savior bore testimony of Himself to the boy prophet. He said, "I am the

---

1. 1835 account. It is possible that it was the Father who bore testimony that Christ was His Son. See the footnote for the summary of the 1835 account in Appendix A.

2. 1832 account.

Lord of glory. I was crucified for the world that all those who believe in my name may have eternal life."[3] What a rare blessing. Undoubtedly the Holy Ghost also testified of the truth of what Joseph was hearing. Thus Joseph received a witness of Christ from every member of the Godhead. His determination to ask of God and his endurance through his struggle with Satan had been richly rewarded. Joseph, the forgiven, also received testimony from all of Deity that Jesus is the Christ, and that He had died for us so that we could live again, eternally.

While there were many things the Savior was about to teach this nascent prophet, within the first few moments of the vision Joseph Smith had already learned things he had not known before entering the grove. He knew that God still answered prayers and was still intimately involved in the lives of His children, a precept that many religious leaders around Joseph disagreed with. He knew that Satan was real and powerful, but at the same time, Joseph knew that God had power over Satan and could deliver His children from that terrible being. Joseph knew that God was a being of unspeakable and inexpressible glory—a being of infinite power. Joseph knew that God brought feelings of indescribable love and delivered immeasurable peace, and that seeing God brought unfathomable joy. Joseph knew that God had a physical body. Joseph knew that God and Christ were two different

---

3. 1832 account; spelling and capitalization standardized.

beings. He knew that God speaks to us through Christ. He knew that God and Christ knew him personally, and that They loved him. Joseph knew that Christ had the power, and the desire, to forgive sins, and that Christ had been crucified for us so that we might gain eternal life. While he may not have consciously thought through each new piece of information, before he had spoken a word to ask a question, Joseph Smith had learned several profound eternal truths.

We know that at some time during this vision many angels appeared, though we do not know when.[4] We can presume, based on the scriptural reports of others who saw God, that these angels probably accompanied the Father and Son. The experience may have been like Lehi's when he saw God sitting on His throne, surrounded by concourses of angels, as Christ descended from the throne to talk with Lehi (see 1 Nephi 1:8). John the Revelator (see Revelation 4:1–11) and Ezekiel (see Ezekiel 1:5–14) reported similar occurrences, as did Isaiah (see Isaiah 6:2–7). Did Joseph see those angels praising God, as they were doing in Lehi's vision? Did they teach Joseph something? We do not have enough information to answer these questions, but as we think of this wonderful event, we may feel to rejoice as those angels must have at the time.[5]

---

4. In the 1835 account, Joseph Smith says, "And I saw many angels in this vision."

5. While it is purely speculation, as long as we remember it is only conjecture, we can perhaps help ourselves picture this real event all

The presence of angels must have made an impression on the young lad, but clearly his mind was most caught up in the two divine beings who had been speaking to him.[6] Having learned who Christ is, and having his immediate concern of forgiveness resolved, Joseph could then gather himself to voice the question he had come to the grove to ask. It took him a moment to overcome the awe

---

the more as we ask ourselves practical questions such as who the angels might have been. Could some of those angels have been the great Book of Mormon prophets who had been waiting so long for this day? Could Mormon and Moroni themselves have been present, witnessing the beginning of the process that would bring their record forth, and rejoicing in it? Could Peter and the Apostles have been there, anxious to see the beginning of the Restoration that would include restoring the keys they had held and the Church they had directed? Could Abraham, Sarah, Isaac, Rebecca, Jacob, Leah, Billah, Zilpah, and Rachel have been there, attending to the event that would lead to the restoration of the covenant that was so important to them? Might Joseph of Egypt have been there to witness the boy he had prophesied of by name? Could Michael himself along with Eve have been there, overseeing the angels who were privy to such a glorious event that would help bring salvation to so many of their children? Because many of these angels must have been among the "noble and great ones," a group which Joseph had presumably been a part of in pre-mortality, could it be that these angels were experiencing a kind of reunion with one whom they regarded as a close friend? And if so, were they rejoicing that their kindred spirit was about to begin his glorious mission, one which they had prophesied of? We cannot know the answers to these questions, but asking them can help us think through the importance of the event that these anonymous angels were witness to.

6. We can presume that this is why the angels are not mentioned in most accounts—because they were not the most important element of the vision and thus usually not necessary to convey what Joseph was trying to teach when he spoke of the experience.

and astonishment at what he was experiencing: this was certainly well beyond the answer he had ever hoped for. Still, before long, Joseph regained his senses and found himself able to respond to his Savior.

Joseph had come to ask which church he should join. It had not yet occurred to him that none of the churches were God's church.[7] He had begun his prayers by asking, "O Lord, what church should I join?"[8] When he got possession of himself again, he repeated the question. He seems to have followed it up with the specific question, "Must I join the Methodist church?"[9] for that was the

---

7. In the 1838 account, as Joseph looks forward to the vision, he speaks of wondering which church he should join or if they were all wrong together (see Joseph Smith—History 1:10). But as he told the specific story, as he came to the part where he would need to recall the specific question he asked God, he was able to clearly recall asking about what church to join because it had not yet occurred to him that they were all wrong (see v. 18). This is common when recalling events at a later date. We think of generalities when thinking of the event as a whole, but when we come to specific details, we are forced to remember the timing and sequence of those details. In recalling the wording of his question, Joseph Smith was reminded of the specific thoughts he had at the time.
8. In the 1843 interview, Joseph Smith says this was his initial question, seemingly even before he was attacked by Satan. He then says he asked that same question again after the Son was introduced to him.
9. This is the question Alexander Neibaur, in his 1844 journal account, recalls the prophet saying he asked. Since we know Joseph Smith was leaning towards Methodism, and since it is unlikely that Neibaur knew that, this seems to be a reasonably probable recollection of the story. Thus I conclude that while the 1843 interview said Joseph first asked what church he should join, he must have also asked if he should join the Methodist church specifically.

church he had been most inclined to align himself with. The answer he got was a surprise.

Joseph was told to join none of the churches. None of them were of God.[10] They were all corrupt.[11] Their creeds were an abomination in the sight of God.[12] The Savior quoted His own prophets, saying that the religious leaders of the day "draw near to me with their lips, but their hearts are far from me, they teach for doctrines the commandments of men, having a form of godliness, but they deny the power thereof" (Isaiah 29:13).[13] Joseph was told that "the world lieth in sin at this time,"[14] and "they have turned aside from the gospel,"[15] had broken the Everlasting Covenant,[16] and had become ungodly. As a result, the anger of the Lord was kindled against the world, and the time that the prophets and apostles had prophesied of was not far distant,[17] for the Savior said, "Lo I come quickly as it is written of me, in the cloud, clothed in the glory of my Father."[18]

---

10. 1842 account; 1840 Orson Pratt account; 1842 Orson Hyde account.

11. 1843 interview.

12. 1838 account.

13. The 1832 account quotes the first part of this scripture. The 1838 account quotes the whole verse as cited here.

14. 1832 account.

15. 1832 account.

16. 1843 Levi Richards account.

17. 1832 account.

18. 1832 account; spelling and punctuation standardized.

The Savior again told Joseph to join none of the churches,[19] commanding him to "go not after them," for God recognized none of them as His own.[20] Joseph was promised that at some point in the future the true doctrine of Christ and the fullness of the gospel would be made known to him.[21] He was to be patient as he waited for that promise to be fulfilled.[22] There may have been a great many more things that the Prophet was told, but this is all that has survived in writing.

There is no doubt that the information was overwhelming. It was simply too much for even a sober-minded and contemplative fourteen-year-old to take in. Undoubtedly, as time went on and he learned more, Joseph came to better appreciate and understand different aspects of this glorious vision. Yet it seems that the answer to his question became the most salient part: he knew he should not join any churches. This was the answer he had gone to the grove to receive, and it was so much on his mind that when he first spoke to his mother after the vision, he immediately told her that he knew her church was not God's church. Moreover, though he had received the answer to his pressing question, he had learned so much more.[23] We will probably never know how much.

---

19. 1838 account.

20. 1842 account; 1840 Orson Pratt account.

21. 1842 account; 1840 Orson Pratt account.

22. 1842 Orson Hyde account.

23. 1838 account.

When the Savior finished teaching the young prophet, the vision withdrew. Though it must have been dramatic and somewhat of a letdown to witness the departure of his divine Father and his Redeemer, Joseph found himself still filled with the Spirit. He had entered the grove in a state of agitation because of his lack of knowledge, but he now felt an indescribable feeling of peace and calm.[24] As he recalled, "My soul was filled with love and for many days I could rejoice with great joy, and the Lord was with me."[25]

Of course the experience was also exhausting. Something about having your nature changed or transfigured so that it can withstand the presence of God must be greatly taxing to a mortal, telestial body. Moses, after experiencing a similar vision, fell to the earth and regained the strength to stand again only after many hours (see Moses 1:10). Though Joseph did not remember how he got there, he found himself sprawled on his back, lying on the ground after the vision closed.[26] He must have collapsed at some point, probably after the withdrawal of the divine. Joseph lay there for some time before he gathered the strength to

---

24. 1840 Orson Pratt account; 1842 Orson Hyde account.

25. 1832 account; punctuation and capitalization standardized.

26. 1838 account. The 1843 interview reads, "When I come to myself, I was sprawling on my back; and it was sometime before my strength returned."

get up.[27] Even after he made his way home, he was so weak that he had to rest on the mantel of the family's cabin, and he looked weary enough that his mother was concerned about him.[28] Somehow his experience had been both energizing and exhausting at the same time.

The weakness Joseph felt did not seem to detract from the feeling of peace, joy, and love that he was engulfed in, for Joseph had seen God. His prayers had been answered. He had been given hope, and that hope would become the hope of mankind. Though most would not believe him,[29] Joseph had seen God—and he knew God had seen him—and that developed a bond and relationship that would see him through ridicule, waiting, pain, and even death. Those who heard Joseph testify of this experience said that they felt more power in hearing him speak of it than at any other point in their lives.[30] So it can be with us. We all can, and should, thrill as we read Joseph's accounts of this vision, and in our minds hear him say, "I saw the Lord."[31]

---

27. The 1844 Alexander Neibaur account says Joseph "endeavored to arise," suggesting he was not able to initially, and that he felt "uncommon feeble" when he made the attempt.

28. 1838 account.

29. The 1832 account says that Joseph Smith could find none that would believe the heavenly vision.

30. Edward Stevenson, *Reminiscences of Joseph, the Prophet, and the Coming Forth of the Book of Mormon* (Salt Lake City: 1893), 4.

31. 1832 account.

A SUMMARY OF
THE ACCOUNTS

When using the firsthand accounts listed here, I take
Joseph Smith at his word. Still, each account includes details that are not in the other accounts, and sometimes it is
difficult to tell how to order the events of one account in
relationship to events that are unique to another account.
Most of the time when we are trying to reconstruct se-
quences, one of two methods enables us to determine the
correct order. Often logical reasoning is enough. Clearly
an attempt to pray vocally had to precede finding that
one's tongue would not work. Also, when reconstructing
possible scenarios, a scenario that can account for all the
data is preferable to one that can account for only some
of it. In any case, if I was ever unable to reconstruct the
sequence with a high degree of confidence, I used tenta-
tive language, such as "probably" or "likely," in order to
indicate that I was presenting an educated supposition.

1832 Account

Joseph first began to write a history of the Church in 1832. Most of it was dictated to a scribe, but the account of the First Vision is in Joseph's own handwriting. It was an unpolished account, but it carries with it more information about Joseph's personal feelings than the other accounts. The following details come from this account:

- Joseph was born in Sharon, Vermont.
- His parents taught him in Christian religion.
- His father's family was poor, and they were required to work hard to economically survive.
- Joseph was concerned for the welfare of his soul at twelve years old.
- Joseph searched the scriptures to find answers to his soul-deep questions.
- Joseph noticed hypocrisy in preachers of religion.
- Joseph pondered and sought answers for three years.
- Joseph felt convicted of his sins.
- Joseph saw that no church matched what he read about in the New Testament.
- Joseph sought God for mercy.
- Joseph saw a "pillar of light" above the brightness of the sun at noonday.
- Joseph was filled with the Spirit of God.
- Joseph saw a divine being.
- Joseph's sins were forgiven.
- The Lord testified to Joseph about His Atonement.

- The Lord quoted Old Testament prophets about the worldwide Apostasy.
- Joseph's soul was filled with love and joy for many days.

1835 Account

This is a brief account given to a man who came to visit Joseph Smith in 1835. One of Joseph's scribes took notes of the account as Joseph told it to his visitor, and Warren Parrish eventually copied it into Joseph's journal. The visitor called himself Joshua the Jewish Minister, though his name was Robert Matthews. Joseph Smith did not place a great deal of trust in this man, and after starting to tell the story of his vision, the Prophet seems to wind it up pretty quickly.

- Joseph wanted to be right before God. He didn't know right or wrong concerning religion.
- Joseph prayed because the Bible told him to ask God.
- Joseph was unable to pray because his tongue was swollen in his mouth.
- Joseph heard a noise behind him in the grove.
- Joseph jumped up on his feet when he heard the noise behind him.
- Joseph's tongue was unbound so he could pray.
- Joseph saw a "pillar of fire."
- Joseph was filled with unspeakable joy.
- Joseph saw a person in the middle of this fire.
- The fire Joseph saw didn't burn anything it touched.

- Joseph saw a second person in the fire.
- Joseph received forgiveness for his sins.
- The Son testified that Jesus Christ is the Son of God.[1]
- Joseph saw many angels.

A few days after this, Joseph was visited by another man, named Erastus Holmes. Joseph also told him of the First Vision, though all that is recorded in Joseph's journal about it is that he spoke of "the first visitation of Angels which was when I was about 14 years old." Though this is short, it is another mention of angels in connection with the First Vision.

1838 Account

In 1838, after the apostasy of several leading brethren, including some who had kept the history of the Church, Joseph Smith started anew to record his history. This became the official history of the Church, and this account of the First Vision is in the Pearl of Great Price.

- Joseph was born in Sharon, Vermont.

---

1. In the account it says that one being appeared, then another, and that "he" told Joseph he was forgiven and that Jesus Christ was the Son of God. The most immediate antecedent for "he" was the second being, which would mean that the Son told Joseph he was forgiven and testified of Himself. If the "he" referred to the first being, it would be somewhat awkward grammatically, but that is not unheard of in this account. We somewhat expect that the Son would tell Joseph he was forgiven and that the Father would testify of the Son. Thus it is difficult to make complete sense of this account.

- Joseph's family moved to Palmyra, New York.
- Joseph listed the names of his family members.
- There was "unusual excitement" about religion in Joseph's area.
- The religious fervor started with the Methodist sect, then spread out among others.
- The churches and converts expressed love for other faiths, but showed otherwise.
- The churches debated and argued with one another with words and opinions.
- Joseph had deep reflections and feelings about all the strife between churches.
- Joseph did not join any of the churches.
- Joseph preferred the Methodist faith over others.
- Joseph read James 1:5, which touched him deeply and forcefully.
- Joseph decided that he could not settle his important questions with the Bible alone.
- Joseph finally concluded that he must ask of God.
- Joseph went to the woods on a clear day in 1820.
- Joseph noted that he had never attempted to pray vocally.
- Joseph noted that he had previously picked a place to pray.
- Joseph knelt and began offering up the desires of his heart to God.
- Joseph was seized upon by a power that bound his tongue.

- Joseph was surrounded by thick darkness.
- Joseph began to lose hope.
- Joseph tried even harder to call upon God for deliverance.
- Joseph was delivered and saw a pillar of light.
- The light gradually descended and fell on Joseph.
- Joseph saw two Personages (so beautiful beyond description).
- The Father called Joseph by name.
- The Father introduced Jesus Christ as His Beloved Son.
- Joseph asked which sect of religion was right.
- Jesus Christ told Joseph that all the sects were wrong.
- Christ quoted Old Testament prophets concerning these false churches and teachers.
- Christ forbade Joseph to join any of the churches.
- Christ taught Joseph other things that he was not allowed to write about.

1842 Account

In 1842, Joseph wrote a letter to John Wentworth, intended to help Wentworth publish something about the Church in his Chicago newspaper and to help Wentworth's friend write a history of Vermont. When neither of those outlets published the account, Joseph Smith printed it in the Church's newspaper.

- Joseph was born in Sharon, Vermont.
- Joseph's family moved to Palmyra, New York.

- Joseph learned about animal husbandry from his father.
- Joseph began reflecting on things of the soul.
- Joseph found a clash in the religious denominations around him.
- Joseph was impacted by James 1:5.
- Joseph went to a grove to pray.
- Joseph's mind was taken away to a higher plane to see a vision.
- Joseph saw two identical personages.
- Joseph saw light brighter than the sun at noonday.
- Joseph was instructed that all churches were teaching incorrect doctrine.
- Joseph was commanded to join no churches.
- Joseph was told that he would receive the fullness of the gospel.

1840 Orson Pratt Account

Orson Pratt made a pamphlet in 1840, wherein he retold the story of Joseph's vision as he remembered hearing it from Joseph, probably on multiple occasions. We can place a great deal of trust in this account because Joseph quoted from it several times in his own 1842 retelling of the vision. Because Joseph Smith relied so much on this account, unless there is a compelling reason not to, I took the information in this account as reliable, for the Prophet was clearly both aware of this account and happy with it.

- Joseph was born in Sharon, Vermont.

- Joseph's family moved to Palmyra, New York.
- Joseph worked on the farm.
- Joseph had limited literary or educational training.
- Joseph had serious reflection on things of eternal value.
- Joseph had deep reflections and feelings about all the strife between churches.
- Joseph realized that there was only one God and that He would not be the author of several conflicting doctrines.
- Joseph attended several denominations to seek knowledge.
- Joseph did not join any of the churches.
- Joseph turned to the Bible for answers.
- Joseph read James 1:5, which touched him deeply and forcefully.
- That scripture seemed to shine a light on his path.
- Joseph was sure he would get an answer about which church had Christ's doctrine.
- Joseph went to a grove.
- Joseph knelt and began to pray.
- Joseph was seized upon by a power of darkness.
- Seeking for help, he was eventually given enough power to start praying again.
- Joseph tried even harder to call upon God in faith.
- Joseph saw a light far away, and saw it descending slowly.
- The light grew brighter as it descended and illuminated the land all around.

- The light was so bright that he expected the trees and leaves around him to catch fire.
- Joseph was encouraged that he would survive when the trees didn't burn.
- Joseph felt a sensation throughout his body.
- Joseph saw two personages.
- The two personages exactly resembled each other.
- Joseph was told his sins were forgiven, which he had been worried about for some time.
- Joseph was told all churches believed in incorrect doctrines and thus were not God's.
- Joseph was told to not go after any of them.
- Joseph was told that in the future, the fullness of the gospel would be given to him.
- After his vision, Joseph was left in a state of peace and calm.

1842 Orson Hyde Account

Orson Hyde made a pamphlet in German for preaching the gospel in Germany. He had also heard the Prophet tell his story a number of times, and his account includes a number of interesting details. His language and that used by the Prophet often mirror each other. The similarity of language between this account and that of Joseph Smith and Orson Pratt lends a great degree of trustworthiness to this account. Orson Hyde was obviously aware of other accounts, and he had certainly heard the story told on occasion. Thus this account is very trustworthy, but still caution needs to be exercised when it introduces a detail not present in another account. Such details were only used in this book if they seemed very harmonious with the ideas presented in other accounts.

- Joseph was born December 23, 1805, in Sharon, Vermont.
- Joseph's family moved to Palmyra, New York.
- Joseph worked on the farm.
- Joseph's education was meager.
- Joseph started thinking seriously about religion.
- Joseph knew that he needed to know the path to heaven before he could try to walk it.
- Joseph recognized errors in the religions around him and saw contradictions in their doctrines.
- Joseph saw hate and contention between all the denominations.
- Joseph recognized that God would have only one path of righteousness.
- Joseph was losing hope of finding the one true doctrine.
- Joseph read James 1:5.
- Joseph knelt and began to pray to God.
- Joseph was attacked by the adversary.
- Joseph's mind was filled with inappropriate images and doubts.
- God delivered Joseph from this attack.
- Joseph was once again able to pray to God.
- The natural world receded from his view.

- Joseph saw two glorious beings who were identical.
- Joseph was instructed to not join any of the churches.
- These churches erred in doctrine, and none were recognized by God as correct.
- Joseph was commanded to wait patiently until the fullness of the gospel would be revealed to him.
- Peace and calm filled Joseph's mind.

1843 Levi Richards Account

In 1843, Levi Richards heard Joseph Smith tell the story of the First Vision and then wrote a summary of it in his journal. This secondhand account does not have the same shared language and use of quotations as the two secondhand accounts listed above. Thus it must be used with caution. At the same time, it does not present much in the way of original data. The most unique thing is that Joseph learned that the everlasting covenant had been broken. Because this mirrors language given to Joseph in Doctrine and Covenants section 1, it seems likely to be accurate.

- Joseph did not know which church to join when he was a youth.
- Joseph entered the grove to ask the Lord which sect was right.
- He was told that none of the churches were right.
- All churches were wrong, and the everlasting covenant was broken.

◆ Earth and hell had opposed and tried to destroy Joseph, but they did not and could not.

1843 Interview

Joseph was interviewed by David Nye White in 1843 for an article for a Pittsburgh newspaper about the Mormons. While some count this as a secondhand source, in reality the Joseph Smith quotation is a firsthand account that was edited by someone else. We cannot tell how much the interview was edited, but it seems likely that the details of the First Vision that made it to publication were not altered or made up by White. Information may have been left out, but it seems very unlikely that White would make up details such as leaving an ax in a stump, for he had no reason to do so. Other details from this edited firsthand account are harmonious with other accounts.

◆ Joseph was fourteen years old when the Lord revealed Himself to Joseph.
◆ Religious denominations around Joseph were going through a reformation.
◆ Joseph was serious about learning which church he should join.
◆ Joseph found James 1:5 and decided to ask God.
◆ Joseph went to a clearing in the woods with a stump with an ax in it.
◆ Joseph prayed and asked which church he should join.

- Joseph saw a pillar of light.
- Joseph saw one personage in the light, and then another.
- One personage said, "Behold my beloved Son, hear him."
- Joseph asked the personage which church he should join.
- Joseph was instructed to join none of them.
- Joseph found himself sprawled on his back.
- Joseph was exhausted and had no strength.

1844 Alexander Neibaur Account

Probably the last time Joseph Smith ever told someone the story of the First Vision was just one month before his death, to Alexander Neibaur. The German Jewish convert went home and wrote the story in his journal. His English was limited, but Neibaur recorded some unique details that are not the kind that would likely be misremembered or created to fill in holes in the story. Additionally, the fact that he recorded it in his journal so soon afterward lends weight to the accuracy of the account. Still, it is a second-hand account, and thus details that are fully unique to it must be approached with caution.

- Joseph attended a revival meeting with his mother, brother, and sister.
- His family got religion, and he wanted to get religion too.

- Joseph felt nothing at the meetings he attended.
- Joseph opened his Bible and was struck by James 1:5.
- Joseph went into the wood to pray.
- Joseph knelt down and his tongue was bound.
- Joseph eventually was released and saw a pillar of fire come down from heaven nearer and nearer.
- Joseph saw a personage in the fire.
- This personage had fair complexion, blue eyes, and a piece of white cloth drawn over his shoulders. His right arm was bare.
- Another personage came to the side of the first personage.
- Joseph asked if he should join the Methodist church.
- He was told no. All have gone astray.
- The personage said, "This is my beloved son hearken ye him."
- The fire came closer to Joseph and rested on him.
- He felt comforted.
- He tried to get up, but was too weak.

THE FULL ACCOUNTS

All of the first- and secondhand accounts have been published online as part of the Joseph Smith Papers Project sponsored by The Church of Jesus Christ of Latter-day Saints. They can easily be found there, but for convenience's sake are also included here.

1832 Account[1]

I was born in the town of Charon [Sharon] in the <State> of Vermont North America on the twenty third day of December AD 1805 of goodly Parents who spared no pains to instruct<ing> me in <the> christian religion[.] at the age of about ten years my Father Joseph Smith Seignior moved to Palmyra Ontario County in the

---

1. "History, circa Summer 1832," The Joseph Smith Papers, https://www.josephsmithpapers.org/paper-summary/history-circa-summer-1832/1, accessed August 31, 2019.

State of New York and being in indigent circumstances were obliged to labour hard for the support of a large Family having nine chilldren and as it required the~~ir~~ exertions of all that were able to render any assistance for the support of the Family therefore we were deprived of the bennifit of an education suffice it to say I was mearly instructtid in reading ~~and~~ writing and the ground <rules> of Arithmatic which const[it]uted my whole literary acquirements. At about the age of twelve years my mind become seriously imprest with regard to the all important concerns ~~of~~ for the wellfare of my immortal Soul which led me to searching the scriptures believeing as I was taught, that they contained the word of God thus applying myself to them and my intimate acquaintance with those of differant denominations led me to marvel excedingly for I discovered that <they did not ~~adorn~~> ~~instead of~~ adorning their profession by a holy walk and Godly conversation agreeable to what I found contained in that sacred depository this was a grief to my Soul thus from the age of twelve years to fifteen I pondered many things in my heart concerning the sittuation of the world of mankind the contentions and divi[si]ons the wicke[d] ness and abominations and the darkness which pervaded the ~~of the~~ minds of mankind my mind become excedingly distressed for I become convicted of my sins and by searching the scriptures I found that ~~mand~~ <mankind> did not come unto the Lord but that they had apostatised from the true and liveing faith and there was no society or denomination that built upon the gospel of Jesus Christ as recorded in the new testament and I felt to mourn for my own sins and for the sins of the world for I learned in the scriptures that God was the same yesterday to day and forever that he was no respecter to persons for he was God for I looked upon the sun the glorious luminary of the earth and also the moon rolling in their magesty through the heavens and also the stars shining in their courses and the earth also upon which I stood and the beast of the field and the fowls of heaven and the fish of the waters and also man walking forth upon the face of the earth in magesty and in the strength of beauty whose power and intiligence in governing the things which are so exceding great and marvilous even in the likeness of him who created h̶i̶m̶ <them> and when I considered upon these things my heart exclaimed well hath the wise man said t̶h̶e̶ <it is a> fool <that>saith in his heart there is no God my heart exclaimed all all these bear testimony and bespeak an omnipotant and omnipreasant power a being who makith Laws and decreeeth and bindeth all things in their bounds who filleth Eternity who was and is and will be from all Eternity to Eternity and when <I> considered all these things and that <that> being seeketh such to worshep him as worship him in spirit and in truth therefore I cried unto the Lord for mercy for there was none else to whom I could go and t̶o̶ obtain mercy and

the Lord heard my cry in the wilderness and while in
<the> attitude of calling upon the Lord <in the 16th year
of my age> a piller of ~~fire~~ light above the brightness of
the sun at noon day come down from above and rested
upon me and I was filled with the spirit of god and the
<Lord> opened the heavens upon me and I saw the Lord
and he spake unto me saying Joseph <my son> thy sins
are forgiven thee. go thy <way> walk in my statutes and
keep my commandments behold I am the Lord of glory
I was crucifyed for the world that all those who believe
on my name may have Eternal life <behold> the world
lieth in sin ~~and~~ at this time and none doeth good no not
one they have turned asside from the gospel and keep not
<my> commandments they draw near to me with their
lips while their hearts are far from me and mine anger is
kindling against the inhabitants of the earth to visit them
acording to thir ungodliness and to bring to pass that
which <hath> been spoken by the mouth of the prophets
and Ap[o]stles behold and lo I come quickly as it [is?]
written of me in the cloud <clothed> in the glory of my
Father and my soul was filled with love and for many days
I could rejoice with great Joy and the Lord was with me
but could find none that would believe the hevnly vision
nevertheless I pondered these things in my heart.

1835 Account[2]

being wrought up in my mind, respecting the subject of religion and looking ~~upon~~ <at> the different systems taught the children of men, I knew not who was right or who was wrong and concidering it of the first importance that I should be right, in matters that involved eternal consequences; being thus perplexed in mind I retired to the silent grove and bowd down before the Lord, under a realising sense that he had said (if the bible be true) ask and you shall receive knock and it shall be opened seek and you shall find and again, if any man lack wisdom let him ask of God who giveth to all men libarally and upbradeth not; information was what I most desired at this time, and with a fixed determination ~~I~~ to obtain it, I called upon the Lord for the first time, in the place above stated or in other words I made a fruitless attempt to pray, my toung seemed to be swolen in my mouth, so that I could not utter, I heard a noise behind me like some person walking towards me, <I> strove again to pray, but could not, the noise of walking seemed to draw nearer, I sprung up on my feet, ~~and~~[p. 23] and looked around, but saw no person or thing that was calculated to produce the noise of walking, I kneeled again my mouth was opened and my toung liberated, and I called on the Lord in mighty

2. "Journal, 1835–1836," p. 23, The Joseph Smith Papers, https://www .josephsmithpapers.org/paper-summary/journal-1835-1836/24, accessed August 31, 2019.

prayer, a pillar of fire appeared above my head, it presently rested down upon ~~my~~ <me> ~~head~~, and filled me with joy unspeakable, a personage appeard in the midst, of this pillar of flame which was spread all around, and yet nothing consumed, another personage soon appeard like unto the first, he said unto me thy sins are forgiven thee, he testifyed unto me that Jesus Christ is the son of God;[70] <and I saw many angels in this vision> I was about 14. years old when I received this first communication;

1838 Account[3]

I was born in the year of our Lord One thousand Eight hundred and five, on the twenty third day of December, in the town of Sharon, Windsor County, State of Vermont. My father Joseph Smith Senior left the State of Vermont and moved to Palmyra, Ontario, (now Wayne) County, in the State of New York when I was in my tenth year.

In about four years after my father's arrival at Palmyra, he moved with his family into Manchester in the same County of Ontario. His family consisting of eleven souls, namely, My Father Joseph Smith, My Mother Lucy Smith whose name previous to her marriage was Mack, daughter of Solomon Mack, my brothers Alvin (who is now

3. "History, circa June 1839–circa 1841 [Draft 2]," p. 2, The Joseph Smith Papers, https://www.josephsmithpapers.org/paper-summary /history-circa-june-1839-circa-1841-draft-2/2, accessed August 31, 2019.

dead) Hyrum, Myself, Samuel Harrison, William, Don Carloss [Carlos], and my Sisters Soph[r]onia, Cathrine [Katharine] and Lucy.

Sometime in the second year after our removal to Manchester, there was in the place where we lived an unusual excitement on the subject of religion. It commenced with the Methodist, but soon became general among all the sects in that region of country, indeed the whole district of Country seemed affected by it and great multitudes united themselves to the different religious parties, which created no small stir and division among the people, Some Crying, "Lo here" and some Lo there. Some were contending for the Methodist faith, Some for the Presbyterian, and some for the Baptist; for notwithstanding the great love which the converts to these different faiths expressed at the time of their conversion, and the great Zeal manifested by the respective Clergy who were active in getting up and promoting this extraordinary scene of religious feeling in order to have every body converted as they were pleased to call it, let them join what sect they pleased[.] Yet when the Converts began to file off some to one party and some to another, it was seen that the seemingly good feelings of both the Priests and the Converts were ~~mere pretence~~ more pretended than real, for a scene of great confusion and bad feeling ensued; Priest contending against priest, and convert against convert so that all their good feelings one for another (if they ever had any) were entirely lost in a strife of words and a contest about opinions.

I was at this time in my fifteenth year. My Fathers family was proselyted to the Presbyterian faith and four of them joined that Church, Namely, My Mother Lucy, My Brothers Hyrum, Samuel Harrison, and my Sister Sophonia.

During this time of great excitement my mind was called up to serious reflection and great uneasiness, but though my feelings were deep and often pungent, still I kept myself aloof from all these parties though I attended their several meetings as occasion would permit. But in process of time my mind became somewhat partial to the Methodist sect, and I felt some desire to be united with them, but so great was the confusion and strife amongst the different denominations that it was impossible for a person young as I was and so unacquainted with men and things to come to any certain conclusion who was right and who was wrong.

My mind at different times was greatly excited for the cry and tumult were so great and incessant. The Presbyterians were most decided against the Baptists and Methodists, and used all their powers of either reason or sophistry to prove their errors, or at least to make the people think they were in error. On the other hand the Baptists and Methodists in their turn were equally Zealous in endeavoring to establish their own tenets and disprove all others.

In the midst of this war of words, and tumult of opinions, I often said to myself, what is to be done? Who of all these parties are right? Or are they all wrong together? and if any one of them be right which is it? And how shall I know it?

While I was laboring under the extreme difficulties caused by the contests of these parties of religionists, I was one day reading the Epistle of James, First Chapter and fifth verse which reads, "If any of you lack wisdom, let him ask of God, that giveth to all men liberally and upbraideth not, and it shall be given him.["] Never did any passage of scripture come with more power to the heart of man that this did at this time to mine. It seemed to enter with great force into every feeling of my heart. I reflected on it again and again, knowing that if any person needed wisdom from God, I did, for how to act I did not know and unless I could get more wisdom than I then had [I] would never know, for the teachers of religion of the different sects understood the same passage of Scripture so differently as <to> destroy all confidence in settling the question by an appeal to the Bible. At length I came to the conclusion that I must either remain in darkness and confusion or else I must do as James directs, that is, Ask of God. I at last came to the determination to ask of God, concluding that if he gave wisdom to them that lacked wisdom, and would give liberally and not upbraid, I might venture. So in accordance with this my determination to ask of God, I retired to the woods to make the attempt. It was on the morning of a beautiful clear day early in the spring of Eightteen hundred and twenty. It was the first time in my life that I had <made> such an attempt, for amidst all <my> anxieties I had never as yet made the attempt to pray vocally.

After I had retired into the place where I had previously designed to go, having looked around me and finding myself alone, I kneeled down and began to offer up the desires of my heart to God, I had scarcely done so, when immediately I was <siezed> upon by some power which entirely overcame me and <had> such astonishing influence over me as to bind my tongue so that I could not speak. Thick darkness gathered around me and it seemed to me for a time as if I were doomed to sudden destruction. But exerting all my powers to call upon God to deliver me out of the power of this enemy which had siezed upon me, and at the very moment when I was ready to sink into despair and abandon myself to destruction, not to an imaginary ruin but to the power of some actual being from the unseen world who had such a marvelous power as I had never before felt in any being. Just at this moment of great alarm I saw a pillar <of> light exactly over my head above the brightness of the sun, which descended ~~gracefully~~ gradually untill it fell upon me. It no sooner appeared than I found myself delivered from the enemy which held me bound. When the light rested upon me I saw two personages (whose brightness and glory defy all description) standing above me in the air. One of <them> spake unto me calling me by name and said (pointing to the other) "This is my beloved Son, Hear him."

My object in going to enquire of the Lord was to know which of all the sects was right, that I might know which to join. No sooner therefore did I get possession of myself so as to be able to speak, than I asked the personages who stood above me in the light, which of all the sects was right, (for at this time it had never entered into my heart that all were wrong) and which I should join. I was answered that I must join none of them, for they were all wrong, and the Personage who addressed me said that all their Creeds were an abomination in his sight, that those professors were all corrupt, that "they draw near to me to with their lips but their hearts are far from me, They teach for doctrines the commandments of men, having a form of Godliness but they deny the power thereof." He again forbade me to join with any of them and many other thing[s] did he say unto me which I cannot write at this time. When I came to myself again I found myself lying on <my> back looking up into Heaven. Some few days after I had this vision I happened to be in company with one of the Methodist Preachers who was very active in the before mentioned religious excitement and conversing with him on the subject of religion I took occasion to give him an account of the vision which I had had. I was greatly surprised at his behaviour, he treated my communication not only lightly but with great contempt, saying it was all of the Devil, that there was no such thing as visions or revelations in these days, that all such things had ceased with the apostles and that there never would be any more of them.

1842 Account[4]

I was born in the town of Sharon Windsor co., Vermont, on the 23d of December, A. D. 1805. When ten years old my parents removed to Palmyra New York, where we resided about four years, and from thence we removed to the town of Manchester.

My father was a farmer and taught me the art of husbandry. When about fourteen years of age I began to reflect upon the importance of being prepared for a future state, and upon enquiring the plan of salvation I found that there was a great clash in religious sentiment; if I went to one society they referred me to one plan, and another to another; each one pointing to his own particular creed as the summum bonum of perfection: considering

---

4. "'Church History,' 1 March 1842," p. 706, The Joseph Smith Papers, https://www.josephsmithpapers.org/paper-summary/church-history-1 -march-1842/1, accessed August 31, 2019.

that all could not be right, and that God could not be the author of so much confusion I determined to investigate the subject more fully, believing that if God had a church it would not be split up into factions, and that if he taught one society to worship one way, and administer in one set of ordinances, he would not teach another principles which were diametrically opposed. Believing the word of God I had confidence in the declaration of James; "If any man lack wisdom let him ask of God who giveth to all men liberally and upbraideth not and it shall be given him," I retired to a secret place in a grove and began to call upon the Lord, while fervently engaged in supplication my mind was taken away from the objects with which I was surrounded, and I was enwrapped in a heavenly vision and saw two glorious personages who exactly resembled each other in features, and likeness, surrounded with a brilliant light which eclipsed the sun at noon-day. They told me that all religious denominations were believing in incorrect doctrines, and that none of them was acknowledged of God as his church and kingdom. And I was expressly commanded to "go not after them," at the same time receiving a promise that the fulness of the gospel should at some future time be made known unto me.

1840 Orson Pratt Account[5]

MR JOSEPH SMITH, jun., who made the following important discovery, was born in the town of Sharon,
Windsor county, Vermont, on the 23d of December, A.D.
1805. When ten years old, his parents, with their family,
moved to Palmyra, New York; in the vicinity of which
he resided for about eleven years, the latter part in the
town of Manchester. Cultivating the earth for a livelihood
was his occupation, in which he employed the most of
his time. His advantages, for acquiring literary knowledge,
were exceedingly small; hence, his education was limited
to a slight acquaintance with two or three of the common
branches of learning. He could read without much difficulty, and write a very imperfect hand; and had a very
limited understanding of the ground rules of arithmetic.
These were his highest and only attainments; while the
rest of those branches, so universally taught in the common schools throughout the United States, were entirely
unknown to him. When somewhere about fourteen or
fifteen years old, he began seriously to reflect upon the
necessity of being prepared for a future state of existence:
but how, or in what way, to prepare himself, was a question, as yet, undetermined in his own mind: he perceived

5. "Appendix: Orson Pratt, A[n] Interesting Account of Several
Remarkable Visions, 1840," The Joseph Smith Papers, https://www
.josephsmithpapers.org/paper-summary/appendix-orson-pratt-an
-interesting-account-of-several-remarkable-visions-1840/3, accessed
August 31, 2019.

that it was a question of infinite importance, and that the salvation of his soul depended upon a correct understanding of the same. He saw, that if he understood not the way, it would be impossible to walk in it, except by chance; and the thought of resting his hopes of eternal life upon chance, or uncertainties, was more than he could endure. If he went to the religious denominations to seek information, each one pointed to its particular tenets, saying—"This is the way, walk ye in it;" while, at the same time, the doctrines of each were, in many respects, in direct opposition to one another. It, also, occurred to his mind, that God was not the author of but one doctrine, and therefore could not acknowledge but one denomination as his church; and that such denomination must be a people, who believe, and teach, that one doctrine, (whatever it may be,) and build upon the same. He then reflected upon the immense number of doctrines, now, in the world, which had given rise to many hundreds of different denominations. The great question to be decided in his mind, was—if any one of these denominations be the Church of Christ, which one is it? Until he could become satisfied, in relation to this question, he could not rest contented. To trust to the decisions of fallible man, and build his hopes upon the same, without any certainty, and knowledge, of his own, would not satisfy the anxious desires that pervaded his breast. To decide, without any positive and definite evidence, on which he could rely, upon a subject involving the future welfare of his soul, was revolting to his feelings. The only alternative, that seemed to be left him, was to read the Scriptures, and endeavour to follow their directions. He, accordingly, commenced perusing the sacred pages of the Bible, with sincerity, believing the things that he read. His mind soon caught hold of the following passage:—"If any of you lack wisdom, let him ask of God, that giveth to all *men* liberally, and upbraideth not; and it shall be given him."—James i. 5. From this promise he learned, that it was the privilege of all men to ask God for wisdom, with the sure and certain expectation of receiving, liberally; without being upbraided for so doing. This was cheering information to him: tidings that gave him great joy. It was like a light shining forth in a dark place, to guide him to the path in which he should walk. He, now, saw that if he inquired of God, there was, not only, a possibility, but a probability; yea, more, a certainty, that he should obtain a knowledge, which, of all the doctrines, was the doctrine of Christ; and, which, of all the churches, was the church of Christ. He, therefore, retired to a secret place, in a grove, but a short distance from his father's house, and knelt down, and began to call upon the Lord. At first, he was severely tempted by the powers of darkness, which endeavoured to overcome him; but he continued to seek for deliverance, until darkness gave way from his mind; and he was enabled to pray, in fervency of the spirit, and in faith. And, while thus pouring out his soul, anxiously desiring an answer from God, he, at length, saw a very bright and glorious light in the heavens above; which, at first, seemed to be at a considerable distance. He continued praying, while the light appeared to be gradually descending towards him; and, as it drew nearer, it increased in brightness, and magnitude, so that, by the time that it reached the tops of the trees, the whole wilderness, for some distance around, was illuminated in a most glorious and brilliant manner. He expected to have seen the leaves and boughs of the trees consumed, as soon as the light came in contact with them; but, perceiving that it did not produce that effect, he was encouraged with the hopes of being able to endure its presence. It continued descending, slowly, until it rested upon the earth, and he was enveloped in the midst of it. When it first came upon him, it produced a peculiar sensation throughout his whole system; and, immediately, his mind was caught away, from the natural objects with which he was surrounded; and he was enwrapped in a heavenly vision, and saw two glorious personages, who exactly resembled each other in their features or likeness. He was informed, that his sins were forgiven. He was also informed upon the subjects, which had for some time previously agitated his mind, viz.—that all the religious denominations were believing in incorrect doctrines; and, consequently, that none of them was acknowledged of God, as his church and kingdom. And he was expressly commanded, to go not after them; and he received a promise that the true doctrine—the fulness of the gospel, should, at some future time, be made known to him; after which, the vision withdrew, leaving his mind in a state of calmness and peace, indescribable.

1842 Orson Hyde German Account (translated into English)[6]

Joseph Smith jun[ior], the person to whom the angel of the Lord was first sent, was born on December 23 in the year of our Lord 1805 in the town of Sharon, Windsor County, Vermont. When he was ten years old, his parents moved to Palmyra in the state of New York. For almost eleven years he lived here [in Palmyra] and in the neighboring town of Manchester. His only occupation was to plow and cultivate the soil. Because his parents were poor and had to feed a large family, his education was meager. He was able to read fairly well, but his ability to write was very limited and had only little literary knowledge. His knowledge of letters did not go any further. Most of the subjects which were generally taught in the United States of America were completely unknown to him at the time he was favored with a heavenly message.

When he had reached his fifteenth year, he began to

---

6. "Orson Hyde, Ein Ruf aus der Wüste (A Cry out of the Wilderness), 1842, extract, English translation," The Joseph Smith Papers, https://www.josephsmithpapers.org/paper-summary/orson-hyde-ein-ruf-aus-der-wste-a-cry-out-of-the-wilderness-1842-extract-english-translation/1, accessed August 31, 2019.

think seriously about the importance of preparing for a future [existence]; but it was very difficult for him to decide how he should go about such an important undertaking. He recognized clearly that it would be impossible for him to walk the proper path without being acquainted with it beforehand; and to base his hopes for eternal life on chance or blind uncertainty would have been more than he had ever been inclined to do.

He discovered the world of religion working under a flood of errors which by virtue of their contradictory opinions and principles laid the foundation for the rise of such different sects and denominations whose feelings toward each other all too often were poisoned by hate, contention, resentment and anger. He felt that there was only one truth and that those who understood it correctly, all understood it in the same way. Nature had endowed him with a keen critical intellect and so he looked through the lens of reason and common sense and with pity and contempt upon those systems of religion, which were so opposed to each other and yet were all obviously based on the scriptures.

After he had sufficiently convinced himself to his own satisfaction that darkness covered the earth and gross darkness [covered] the nations, the hope of ever finding a sect or denomination that was in possession of unadulterated truth left him.

Consequently he began in an attitude of faith his own

investigation of the word of God [feeling that it was] the best way to arrive at a knowledge of the truth. He had not proceeded very far in this laudable endeavor when his eyes fell upon the following verse of St. James [1:5]: "If any of you lack wisdom, let him ask of God, that giveth to all men liberally, and upbraideth not; and it shall be given him." He considered this scripture an authorization for him to solemnly call upon his creator to present his needs before him with the certain expectation of some success. And so he began to pour out to the Lord with fervent determination the earnest desires of his soul. On one occasion, he went to a small grove of trees near his father's home and knelt down before God in solemn prayer. The adversary then made several strenuous efforts to cool his ardent soul. He filled his mind with doubts and brought to mind all manner of inappropriate images to prevent him from obtaining the object of his endeavors; but the overflowing mercy of God came to buoy him up and gave new impetus to his failing strength. However, the dark cloud soon parted and light and peace filled his frightened heart. Once again he called upon the Lord with faith and fervency of spirit.

At this sacred moment, the natural world around him was excluded from his view, so that he would be open to the presentation of heavenly and spiritual things. Two glorious heavenly personages stood before him, resembling each other exactly in features and stature. They told him that his prayers had been answered and that the Lord had decided to grant him a special blessing. He was also told that he should not join any of the religious sects or denominations, because all of them erred in doctrine and none was recognized by God as his church and kingdom. He was further commanded, to wait patiently until some future time, when the true doctrine of Christ and the complete truth of the gospel would be revealed to him. The vision closed and peace and calm filled his mind.

1843 Levi Richards Account[7]

Pres. J. Smith bore testimony to the same—saying that when he was a youth he began to think about these ~~these~~ things but could not find out which of all the sects were right—he went into the grove & enquired of the Lord which of all the sects were right—re received for answer that none of them were right, that they were all wrong, & that the Everlasting covena[n]t was broken= he said he understoood the fulness of the Gospel from beginning to end

1843 Interview[8]

The Lord does reveal himself to me. I know it. He revealed himself to me first when I was about fourteen

7. "Levi Richards, Journal, 11 June 1843, extract," The Joseph Smith Papers, https://www.josephsmithpapers.org/paper-summary/levi-richards-journal-11-june-1843-extract/1, accessed August 31, 2019.
8. "Interview, 21 August 1843, extract," p. [3], The Joseph Smith Papers, https://www.josephsmithpapers.org/paper-summary/interview-21-august-1843-extract/1

years old, a mere boy. I will tell you about it. There was a reformation among the different religious denominations in the neighborhood where I lived, and I became serious, and was desirous to know what Church to join. While thinking of this matter, I opened the Testament promiscuously on these words, in James, 'Ask of the Lord who giveth to all men liberally and upbraideth not.' I just determined I'd ask him. I immediately went out into the woods where my father had a clearing, and went to the stump where I had stuck my axe when I had quit work, and I kneeled down, and prayed, saying, 'O Lord, what Church shall I join.' Directly I saw a light, and then a glorious personage in the light, and then another personage, and the first personage said to the second, "Behold my beloved Son, hear him." I then, addressed this second person, saying, "O Lord, what Church shall I join." He replied, "don't join any of them, they are all corrupt." The vision then vanished, and when I come to myself, I was sprawling on my back; and it was sometime before my strength returned. When I went home and told the people that I had a revelation, and that all the churches were corrupt, they persecuted me, and they have persecuted me ever since.

1844 Alexander Neibaur Account[9]

Br Joseph tolt us the first call he had a Revival Meeting his Mother & Br & Sister got Religion, he wanted to get Religion too wanted to feel & shout like the Rest but could feel nothing, opened his Bible the first Passage that struck him was if any man lack Wisdom let him ask of God who giveth to all Men liberallity & upbraidet not went into the Wood to pray kneelt himself down his tongue was closet cleavet to his roof—could utter not a word, felt easier after a while= saw a fire towards heaven came near & nearer saw a personage in the fire light complexion blue eyes a piece of white cloth drawn over his shoulders his right arm bear after a w[h]ile a other person came to the side of the first Mr Smith then asked must I join the Methodist Church= No= they are not my People, th all have gone astray there is none that doeth good no not one, but this is my Beloved son harken ye him, the fire drew nigher Rested upon the tree enveloped him *[illegible]* comforted Indeavoured to arise but felt uncomen feeble= got into the house told the Methodist priest, said this was not a age for God to Reveal himself in Vision Revelation has ceased with the New Testament.

9. "Alexander Neibaur, Journal, 24 May 1844, extract," p. [23], The Joseph Smith Papers, https://www.josephsmithpapers.org/paper -summary/alexander-neibaur-journal-24-may-1844-extract/1, accessed August 31, 2019.

ABOUT THE AUTHOR

KERRY MUHLESTEIN is a professor and former associate chair of the Department of Ancient Scripture at Brigham Young University, where he has taught about the First Vision for over two decades. He is also the director of research for that department. He has taught in the history department of three universities and has been part of award-winning history publications. He received his BS in psychology with a Hebrew minor from BYU, his MA in Ancient Near Eastern studies from BYU, and his PhD from UCLA in Egyptology. He is also the director of the BYU Egypt Excavation Project. He and his wife, Julianne, are the parents of six children, and they have lived in Jerusalem on multiple occasions while Kerry taught there.